Teaching English in Primary Schools

A Handbook of Teaching Strategies for Literacy

David Wray and **Jane Medwell**

Letts EDUCATIONAL

Aldine Place
London
W12 8AW

Tel: 0181-740 2268
Fax: 0181-743 8451
e-mail: he@lettsed.co.uk

A CIP catalogue record is available from the British Library

ISBN 1-85805-319-6
Copyright David Wray and Jane Medwell © 1998

Reprinted 1998

Designed and edited by Topics – The Creative Partnership, Exeter

Printed and bound in Great Britain by Progressive Printing (UK) Ltd, Leigh-on-Sea, Essex

Contents

Monitoring children's progress in primary English

Resource sheets

About the series

The Letts QTS Series offers support for all those preparing to become teachers and working towards Qualified Teacher Status (QTS). The content, teaching approaches and practical ideas are useful for trainee teachers, teacher tutors and mentors, as well as for practising teachers and teacher educators in higher education.

The Letts QTS Series addresses the new standards for QTS and the content of the Initial Teacher Training National Curriculum (ITTNC). These are central to the improvement of standards in schools. The series is specifically designed to help all trainee teachers cover the content of the ITTNC and achieve the national standards in order to be awarded QTS.

The short series handbook *QTS: A Practical Introduction* gives trainees an overview of the QTS requirement and a more detailed interpretation of each standard.

The other books in the Letts QTS Series offer trainees the chance to audit their knowledge of the content of the subjects in the ITTNC, pinpoint areas of further work, and use support materials to develop their knowledge. The first two subjects addressed are English and Mathematics for primary teachers.

There are two Letts QTS Series books for each subject:

Book 1 addresses trainees' subject knowledge at their own level by offering a systematic and comprehensive guide to the subject knowledge requirements of the ITTNC. Trainees can check their own knowledge of the subject against that specified in the ITTNC. Section one provides a comprehensive **audit** of this subject knowledge and understanding, with helpful **feedback** and follow-up set out in section two. Having identified areas of subject knowledge for attention, trainees can then use the support materials in section three to develop **key ideas** and map out their **personal learning plan**.

Book 2 for each subject is a handbook of **lesson plans**, **knowledge** and **methods**. This provides details of carefully selected lessons which illustrate effective teaching. It shows how lesson planning and classroom teaching draw on a high level of subject knowledge. It demonstrates how carefully integrated whole-class teaching and group and individual work can be designed to ensure that pupils make progress in their learning.

There is also a tutor-support pack for each subject.

The Letts QTS Series aims to break down the requirements of QTS into manageable units so that trainees can evaluate and improve their knowledge of each subject.

The books in the series are written in a straightforward way by authors who are all experienced teachers, teacher educators, researchers, writers and specialists in their subject areas.

Titles on Information Technology and Science for primary teachers will follow, together with titles for trainees preparing to teach in the secondary phase of schooling.

About this book

The teaching of English to primary pupils is currently undergoing some major changes, especially with regard to the teaching of literacy. The National Literacy Strategy makes a number of demands on schools in terms of teaching approaches in reading and writing and, by extension, speaking and listening. Perhaps the most salient of these changes is the introduction of a literacy hour into primary schools – that is, an hour per day dedicated to the teaching of reading and writing. Not only is an hour a day now prescribed for literacy teaching, there is also some very firm guidance about what the contents of that hour should be and for many teachers this will

involve a very real change to their classroom practices.

One of the major purposes of this book is to offer some practical suggestions on managing and teaching the literacy hour. The emphasis here is on the practical and the larger part of the book is dedicated to lesson plans and teaching suggestions related to this hour. Also provided are a number of resources, which can be used more or less without change in the classroom, with children of a range of ages and abilities.

Additionally, the book is concerned to set these practical suggestions within a

coherent framework of current ideas about the teaching and learning of literacy. Consequently we begin the book by outlining some key ideas about the ways that children learn literacy and therefore the ways in which teachers can best teach them.

It is hoped that this book will prove a useful source of ideas and inspiration to teachers and would-be teachers of literacy.

Learning and teaching literacy: a framework of essential ideas

From learning to teaching

Understanding learning is the key to effective teaching

Developing effective teaching of any subject would be impossible without a thorough understanding of learning. Children's learning is the intended outcome of all teaching and, while it would not be true to say that we currently know everything there is to know about learning, we have amassed over the past decades a great deal of soundly based knowledge about learning and the learning process. This knowledge has come partly from scientific research, often conducted in laboratories and under clinical conditions (the work of Piaget is one example of this) but also validated and extended by work in real classrooms (much of Bruner's work, for example). It has also been enriched by theoretical developments which have changed the ways we commonly think about learning (Vygotsky's insights are perhaps the best example of this). The main purpose of this section of the book is to outline current insights into the process of learning and then to try to apply these to teaching. On the basis of this application we will then describe some principles which underpin the teaching of literacy.

The section will then go on to outline what it is that primary children are now expected to learn in English, a body of knowledge and skills which is becoming more and more tightly specified by successive waves of educational reform. Finally, it will outline what beginning teachers are expected to understand and be able to do in terms of teaching primary English, according to the latest requirements. (What beginning primary teachers are expected to know about English was dealt with in some depth in the companion volume to this one, *English for Primary Teachers*.)

Key ideas about learning

Some insights into learning

Four basic insights into the nature of the learning process have come from research over the past decade or so. Each of these has important implications for approaches to teaching.

Learning proceeds from the known to the unknown.

Learning is a process of interaction between what is known and what is to be learnt
It has become quite clear that, in order to do any real learning, we have to draw upon knowledge we already have about a subject. The more we know about the subject, the more likely it is that we shall learn any given piece of knowledge. Brown (1979) has described this as

'headfitting', by which is simply meant that the closer the distance between what is already known by the learner and the particular information to be learnt, the more likely it is that learning will be successful. Learning which does not make connections with our prior knowledge is learning at the level of rote only, and is soon forgotten once deliberate attempts to remember it have stopped. (Most people can remember times they learnt material in this way, usually as preparation for some kind of test: once the test was over, the information 'went out of their heads'.)

Learning can be defined as 'the expansion and modification of existing ways of conceiving the world in the light of alternative ways' (Wray & Medwell, 1991, p. 9). Such a constructivist approach to learning places great emphasis upon the ways in which prior knowledge is structured in the learner's mind and in which it is activated during learning. Theories about this are generally known as *schema* theories as they hypothesize that knowledge is stored in our minds in patterned ways (*schemata*) (Rumelhart, 1980). Such theories suggest that learning depends, firstly, upon the requisite prior knowledge being in the mind of the learner and, secondly, upon it being brought to the forefront of the learner's mind. According to Rumelhart (1980) there are three major processes by which existing *schemata* are altered. Accretion is the acquisition of new knowledge that simply fits into pre-existing schemata. In restructuring, existing schemata are reorganized to give new insights, and in tuning existing skills and knowledge structures are made increasingly automatic. These three processes operate in conjunction to make up learning.

> The idea of memory and knowledge being organized in our minds into schemata is not a new one, of course. It goes back to Bartlett's work in the 1930s and Piaget's theories of cognitive development.

Schema theories also suggest that the ways in which individuals learn, and the precise content of what they learn, are different for each person, since no two people will have exactly the same schema about a particular phenomenon. An excellent example of this comes from two interesting experiments carried out by Pichert and Anderson (1977) that suggest that a reader's prior 'mind-set' and purpose for reading can influence in a surprising way the amount of information he or she remembers from reading a text. They asked students to read a passage in which there were approximately the same numbers of references to features likely to interest a prospective house buyer or a prospective burglar. The passage is given overleaf. Some students were asked to read the passage from the point of view of a burglar and some from the point of view of a house buyer. All the students were later asked to recall all they could of the passage. There was a significant difference between the kind of ideas remembered by each group, each student recalling more details which fitted his/her mind-set. Later the students were asked to cast their minds back to the passage and given a new perspective from which to look at it. It was found that they were then able to recall ideas that previously had been impossible to recall. These results suggest that a reader's schema substantially influences what a reader remembers of a text and that changing this schema in itself alters what is remembered.

> Schema research also suggests that the assumption that children will all learn the same things simply through their teachers telling them is rather misguided.

Learning is a social process

Ideas about learning have progressed significantly away from Piaget's purely 'lone scientist' view of learners as acting upon their environments, observing the results and then, through reflection,

8

THE HOUSE PASSAGE

The two boys ran until they came to the driveway. "See, I told you today was good for skipping school," said Mark. "Mum is never home on Thursday," he added. Tall hedges hid the house from the road so the pair strolled across the finely landscaped yard. "I never knew your place was so big," said Pete. "Yeah, but it's nicer now than it used to be since Dad had the new stone siding put on and added the fireplace."

There were front and back doors and a side door which led to the garage which was empty except for three parked 10-speed bikes. They went in the side door, Mark explaining that it was always open in case his younger sisters got home earlier than their mother.

Pete wanted to see the house so Mark started with the living room. It, like the rest of the downstairs, was newly painted. Mark turned on the stereo, the noise of which worried Pete. "Don't worry, the nearest house is a quarter of a mile away," Mark shouted. Pete felt more comfortable observing that no houses could be seen in any direction beyond the huge yard.

The dining room, with all the china, silver and glass, was no place to play so the boys moved into the large kitchen where they made sandwiches. Mark said they wouldn't go to the basement because it had been damp and musty ever since the new plumbing had been installed.

"This is where my Dad keeps his famous paintings and his coin collection," Mark said as they peered into the study. Mark bragged that he could get spending money whenever he liked since he'd discovered that his Dad kept a lot in the desk drawer.

There were three upstairs bedrooms. Mark showed Pete his mother's wardrobe which was filled with furs and the locked box which held her jewels. His sister's room was uninteresting except for the colour TV which Mark carried to his room. Mark bragged that the bathroom in the hall was his since one had been added to his sister's room. The big highlight in his room, though, was a leak in the ceiling where the old roof had finally rotted.

From individual to social views of learning

modifying or fine-tuning their schema concerning these environments. Modern learning theory gives much greater recognition to the importance of social interaction and support and posits a view of the learner as a social constructor of knowledge. In collaboration with others, learners establish:

• Shared consciousness
A group working together can construct knowledge to a higher level than can the individuals in that group each working separately. The knowledge rests upon the group interaction.

• Borrowed consciousness
Individuals working alongside more knowledgeable others can 'borrow' their understanding of tasks and ideas to enable them to work successfully. Vygotsky has termed the gap between what a learner can do in collaboration with others and what he/she can do alone, the 'zone of proximal development' and suggests that all learning in fact occurs twice in the learner: once on the social plane and once on the individual.

> Most learning theorists nowadays would admit to having been significantly influenced by the ideas of Vygotsky.

Situated cognition	**Learning is a situated process** We learn everything in a context. That is not a controversial statement. But modern learning theorists go further than this and suggest that what we learn is the context as much as any skills and processes which we use within that context (Lave & Wenger, 1991). In other words the knowledge and skill we acquire through learning is only usable in a context very similar to that in which it was learnt. Psychologists have sought in vain for 'generalizable skills'; skills that once learnt could be applied in a variety of contexts. Claims about generalizability were once made for the teaching of such subjects as Latin, which, it was argued, gave learners a mental discipline that would benefit their learning in other areas. Similar claims are currently made for the learning of such things as 'thinking skills' and other 'personal transferable skills' such as the ability to study effectively. Learning theory provides a very shaky basis for such developments and 'situated cognition' comes much closer to explaining some of the observable problems children have in learning.

One of the most familiar of these problems is that of transfer of learning. Why is it that a child who spells ten words correctly in a spelling test is likely to spell several of these wrongly when writing a story a short while afterwards? The answer is simply that the learning of the spelling is so inextricably bound up with the context of learning that it cannot easily be applied outside of this context.

There are many instances of this, which will be familiar to most teachers. In a class taught by one of us, for example, there was a boy who was an expert at quoting horse-racing odds but could not manage school 'sums' although the mathematical content of these was actually much simpler. Similarly, many tradesmen like decorators, carpenters and plumbers have to perform very complex mathematical calculations as part of their everyday jobs yet for many mathematics would have been an area of some difficulty when at school. Medwell (1993) reports how, in her research into children's writing, she found one girl who showed no evidence at all of drafting or revising in her school writing and showed no awareness of this when talking about her writing. She was, however, the organizer of a club for her friends at home and had produced a written set of club rules, which showed a number of signs of having been revised. She had certainly not transferred her understanding from one context to another.

Beyond cognition to awareness	**Learning is a metacognitive process** A good deal of interest has been aroused by the notion that the most effective learners are those who have a degree of awareness about their own levels of understanding of what they are learning. Vygotsky suggested (1962) that there are two stages in the development of knowledge: firstly, its automatic unconscious acquisition (we learn things or how to do things, but we do not know that we know these things), and secondly, a gradual increase in active conscious control over that knowledge (we begin to know what we know and that there is more that we do not know). This distinction is essentially the difference between the cognitive and metacognitive aspects of knowledge and thought. The term metacognition is used to refer to the deliberate conscious control of one's own cognitive actions (Brown, 1980).

Numerous research studies have examined the operation of metacognition during the reading process in both children and adults. Key questions have been how successful are readers at monitoring their own comprehension during reading and are there any differences in this monitoring between readers of various levels of maturity and ability. Overall, there have been remarkable consistencies in the findings of these studies and the two most replicated results have been that:

> *Younger and poorer readers have little awareness that they must attempt to make sense of text; they focus on reading as a decoding process, rather than as a meaning-getting process* (Baker & Brown, 1984, p.358)

> *Younger children and poorer readers are unlikely to demonstrate that they notice major blocks to text understanding. They seem not to realize when they do not understand* (Garner & Reis, 1981, p.571).

Arising from such work there has been a strong suggestion that learning can be improved by increasing learners' awareness of their own mental processes and some teaching strategies have been developed which place deliberate emphasis on learners' metacognition.

> Anyone who has observed a child reading aloud from a text more or less perfectly and then being unable to describe what the text was about will recognize that young children are often not aware of their own thought processes.

Principles for teaching

From learning to teaching

Some clear principles for teaching emerge from these insights into learning. These have relevance across the curriculum but are particularly important when considering the teaching of literacy and language.

Teachers need to ensure that learners have sufficient previous knowledge and/or understanding to enable them to learn the new things planned for them. They also need to help learners make explicit the links between what they already know and what they are currently learning.

Teachers need to make provision for group interaction and discussion as part of their teaching, giving children opportunities to engage in guided work both in small, teacher-less groups and in groups working alongside experts. For group interaction truly to take place, and to be beneficial in learning, the activities planned for children need to demand more than that they simply sit together: they have to be planned so that discussion is an essential part of them.

Teachers need to ensure meaningful and appropriate contexts for learning, particularly in basic literacy skills. Children should be taught the skills they need in settings that are as close as possible to those in which those skills are regularly used. Decontextualized exercises, for example, are not likely to be effective as a long-term teaching strategy.

Teachers should try to promote learners' knowledge and awareness of their own thinking and learning. This might be done, for example, by encouraging them to think aloud as they perform particular cognitive tasks. It will also be achieved through the essential teaching strategy of teacher demonstration.

> Teacher demonstration, or modelling, is a key teaching strategy with all kinds of uses.

Towards a model for teaching

Palincsar & Brown (1984) describe a teaching procedure that begins from the principles just outlined. Working with the aim of improving students' abilities to respond effectively to text, they begin by arguing that most attempts to train students to do this have produced rather discouraging outcomes. Teaching has apparently had little real impact upon learners' use of strategies for making sense of textual materials and, particularly, on the transfer of these strategies to activities outside those directly experienced during the teaching context. This failure to effect real change in learners' approaches to dealing with text they attribute to a model of learning which sees learners as simply responding, relatively passively, to instruction without really being made aware of just what they are learning and why. They claim that teaching, to be successful, needs to encourage learners to be active in their use of strategies and to understand why, and when, they should use the strategies to which they have been introduced.

The model of teaching they propose as an alternative is based upon the twin ideas of 'expert scaffolding' and what they refer to as 'proleptic' teaching: that is, teaching in anticipation of competence. This model arises from the ideas of Vygotsky (1978), who put forward the notion that children first experience a particular cognitive activity in collaboration with expert practitioners. The child is firstly a spectator as the expert (parent or teacher) does the majority of the cognitive work. He then becomes a novice as he starts to take over some of the work under the close supervision of the expert. As the child grows in experience and capability of performing the task, the expert passes over greater and greater responsibility but still acts as a guide, assisting the child at problematic points. Eventually, the child assumes full responsibility for the task with the expert present still in the role of a supportive audience.

Using this approach to teaching, children learn about the task at their own pace, joining in only at a level at which they are capable – or perhaps a little beyond this level so that the task continually provides sufficient challenge to be interesting. The approach is often referred to as an apprenticeship approach and most primary teachers will be familiar with its operation in the teaching of reading (Waterland, 1985). In the apprenticeship approach to reading, the teacher and child begin by sharing a book together with, at first, most of the actual reading being done by the teacher. As the child develops confidence through repeated sharings of the book, he/she gradually takes over the reading until the teacher can withdraw entirely.

The zone of proximal development

The distance between the level at which children can manage independently and at which they can manage with the aid of an expert is termed by Vygotsky 'the zone of proximal development'. This, according to the model of teaching that has begun to emerge from these ideas, is the area in which the most profitable instruction can proceed. Vygotsky claimed that 'what children can do with the assistance of others might be in some sense even more indicative of their mental development than what they can do alone' (1978, p.85). What they can do collaboratively today becomes what they can do independently tomorrow.

Most of us will have had experience of being taught in this way, even if those teaching us could not explain their pedagogical theory in these terms. I learnt to drive a car by sitting alongside an expert driver who had over-riding control of the driving mechanisms (the pedals) and was operating these, without my knowledge, to make sure I did nothing likely to dent my confidence. I taught my daughter to swim by walking alongside her in the water and holding her around the middle while she kicked and splashed her arms. Eventually I began to let go for seconds at a time, then minutes, until finally she set off across the pool entirely unaided.

> Apprenticeship at its most effective involves more than just demonstrations. It also involves providing the learner with a model of how to think through particular actions.

Looking more closely at apprenticeship

There appear to be four stages to the teaching process implied by the model: demonstration, joint activity, supported activity, and individual activity.

Demonstration

During this stage, the expert models the skilful behaviour being taught by demonstrating it in action. Thus a teacher might read to a group of children from an enlarged text which they can all see clearly. An important function of this shared reading is to provide a model to the children of how such a text can be read. The teacher therefore ensures that she shows such features of reading as:

- moving from left to right and top to bottom
- reading the words rather than the pictures
- predicting what might be coming next
- using book features such as an index in an information book, etc.

There is some evidence that learning can be assisted if this modelling is accompanied by a commentary from the expert during which her thinking about the activities being undertaken is made explicit. One relatively simple procedure is that of the teacher modelling how she tackles the skills she is teaching, that is, reading or writing in such a way that the learners have access to the thought processes which accompany these activities. Tonjes (1988) discusses metacognitive modelling as a way of teachers demonstrating to children the reading and comprehension monitoring strategies which they use and argues that teachers using this approach should concentrate upon modelling mental processes – what they think as they read or write – rather than simply procedures – what they do. Only in this way, she suggests, can children learn strategies that they can apply across a range of situations rather than believe that those strategies are limited to the context in which they were encountered.

Joint activity

The expert and the learner share the activity. This may begin by the expert retaining responsibility for the difficult parts while the learner takes on the easy parts, while in some teaching strategies prior agreement is reached that participants will take turns at carrying out sections of the activity. The expert is always on hand to take full control if necessary. One of the best examples of this joint activity is that known as 'paired reading' (Morgan, 1986) in which the teacher (or parent) and the learner read aloud in unison until the learner signals that he/she is ready to go it alone. The teacher withdraws from the reading but is ready to rejoin if the learner shows signs of difficulty such as prolonged pausing or reading errors.

Supported activity

The learner undertakes the activity alone, but under the watchful eye of the expert who is always ready to step in if necessary. This can be the stage in the process that is most often neglected and it has been suggested (Wray & Lewis, 1997) that teachers tend to move too rapidly from heavily supporting children's work to asking them to work without support. Consequently, it is at this stage that there appears to be most need of practical teaching strategies. We shall briefly describe several of these later in the book.

> Ideally teaching should move gradually from the teacher taking entire responsibility for the thinking towards control of this passing over to the children. However, this can be rather difficult to manage in a crowded classroom.

Individual activity

The learner assumes sole responsibility for the activity. Some learners will, of course, move much more rapidly to this stage than others and the teacher needs to be sensitive to this. It is, arguably, equally as damaging to hold back learners by insisting they go through the same programme of support and practice as everyone else as it is to rush learners through such a programme when they need a more extensive programme of support.

The model in action

Reciprocal teaching

A set of teaching procedures based upon this apprenticeship model was designed by Palincsar & Brown (1984) to try to develop the reading and comprehension monitoring of a group of eleven-year-olds with reading problems. Their approach used what they termed 'reciprocal teaching' to focus upon four activities:

> Comprehension monitoring is the ability to recognize one's problems in understanding and then to act to address those problems.

- summarizing – asking the children to summarize sections of text, thereby encouraging them to focus upon the main ideas in a passage and to check their own understanding of these

- questioning – getting the children to ask questions about what they read, again encouraging them to attend to the principal ideas and to think about their own comprehension of these

- clarifying – asking the children to clarify potentially problematic sections of text, requiring them to evaluate the current state of their understanding

- predicting – getting them to go beyond the words of the text to make inferences which they must justify by reference to what they read.

Each of these activities had a cognitive and a metacognitive dimension in that not only were the children working upon their comprehension of the texts (comprehension fostering) but they were also having to reflect upon the extent of their comprehension (comprehension monitoring).

The reciprocal teaching procedure involved an interactive 'game' between the teacher and the learners in which each took it in turns to lead a dialogue about a particular section of text. The 'teacher' for each section first asked a question, then summarized, then clarified and predicted as appropriate. The real teacher modelled each of these activities and the role played by the children was gradually expanded as time went on from mostly pupil to mostly teacher.

This procedure was tested on a group of eleven-year-olds with reading difficulties. These children initially had trouble in taking over the role of teacher and needed a good deal of help in verbalizing during summarizing, questioning, clarifying and predicting. They did eventually, however, become much more accomplished leaders of the comprehension dialogues and showed a very significant improvement on tests of reading comprehension, an improvement which seemed to generalize to other classroom activities and did not fade away after the completion of the research project. Palincsar & Brown attribute the success of their teaching programme to the reciprocal teaching procedure. They suggest that it involved extensive modelling of comprehension fostering and monitoring strategies which are usually difficult to detect in expert readers, that it forced children to take part in dialogues about their understanding even if at a non-expert level and that they learnt from this engagement.

Gilroy & Moore (1988) report on the results of their replication of the Palincsar & Brown reciprocal-teaching procedure with nine- to thirteen-year-olds in New Zealand. They found that these children made positive gains in comprehension test scores. In a review of research on the reciprocal teaching approach Moore (1988) agrees with the Palincsar & Brown analysis of the strengths of the approach and suggests that it has a great deal to offer, particularly to children with identifiable weaknesses in reading comprehension.

Meta-reading

As an example of this approach, examine the following extract from one teaching episode. The class was doing some work on the topic of 'Engines' and the teacher had introduced them to a book about this topic. She began by sharing a photocopied extract from the book with a group of children. She accompanied her reading of this text by a commentary explaining her thinking as she worked with its ideas. Here is the first part of her reading (the words highlighted are directly read from the text):

> *Now, this passage is called* **The Steam Engine**. *I hope it might tell me something about how steam engines work and perhaps about how they were invented. I know that James Watt made the first steam engine. I suppose the passage might tell me when this happened. I'll read the first sentence or so.* **The power developed by steam has fascinated people for hundreds of years. During the first century AD, Greek scientists realized that steam contained energy that could possibly be used by people.** *Oh, it looks like the power of steam has been known about for longer than I thought.* **The first century AD** – *that's around 1800 years ago. I'm not sure what it means about steam containing energy though. I'd better read carefully to try to find that out.*

During this meta-reading, the teacher was concentrating on doing four kinds of things. She was:

- predicting – looking forward to the information the text might give her

- clarifying – working out ideas in ways she could better understand them

- questioning – allowing the text to spark off further questions in her mind

- summarizing – putting the information in the text into a few words.

These four activities were discussed explicitly with the group and written on large cards, which were then displayed in the classroom. Later, with a different passage, the teacher agreed with the group that they would take it in turns to predict what the passage might be going to be about, to clarify what it told them, to ask questions about what they read and to summarize what they learnt.

Later still, the group was given the task of reading a passage amongst themselves using the same strategies to guide their discussion.

The ultimate aim, of course, was that they would become sufficiently familiar with this procedure for interacting with a text that they were able to adopt it when reading for themselves. What they learnt as a social activity would become internalized and individual.

Extending the scaffolding

Supporting learners

As mentioned above, there appears to be a tendency for teachers to withdraw too quickly the support (scaffolding) they offer to learners who are struggling to master new skills. There is a clear need for teachers to develop a range of ways in which learners might be given support without the necessity for the teacher to be constantly with them, which, of course, is impossible. We shall describe here just two examples of support structures – KWL grids and writing frames – that have proved particularly useful in helping readers to find and use information from non-fiction texts. Further examples of such scaffolding will be given later in the book.

See Wray & Lewis, 1997, for more information about these strategies.

KWL grids

The KWL grid was developed as a teaching strategy in the USA (Ogle, 1989) and is a simple but effective strategy which both takes readers

What do I KNOW about this topic?	What do I WANT to know?	What have I LEARNT?
They had wars They had maps They had dogs long ships They lived in straw houses They had fleas They had helmets. They sailed all over England They had shields	Why did they sail all over England? Why did they have horns on there helmets? Why did they have dogs?	

This example of a partially completed KWL grid was produced by a group of Year 4 children beginning a topic on the Vikings.

through the steps of the research process and also records their learning. It gives a logical structure for tackling research tasks in many areas of the curriculum and it is this combination of simplicity and logic that seems to be so useful to readers with learning difficulties. A KWL grid consists of three columns, the first two of which set the scene for the reading by requiring thought about prior knowledge and just what the reader predicts he/she might learn from the material to be read. The third column acts as a note-taking space.

There seem to be two major benefits from use of this strategy. Firstly, because it begins with the reader's knowledge, it makes the copying out of large sections from the text very unlikely. Most teachers of junior-aged children will recognize the copying phenomenon as one of their biggest problems in teaching children to read for information, an observation that is probably not confined to that age group.

Secondly, it seems that children readily recognize the usefulness of the strategy. Wray & Lewis (1997) give examples of children who, having been introduced to the KWL strategy, continue to use it independently because they see its usefulness. Most of these children, in fact, have reading problems and for them the very significant improvement in 'research' work that the KWL inspires is an important motivator.

See *Resource sheets* for a blank KWL grid that you might use with children.

Writing frames

In our group we had a discussion about whether it was a good idea to build a new supermarket in the field beside our school.

Some people thought it was a good idea because if you needed something after school. If you needed some milk you only a couple of yards away.

Others thought it was a bad idea because the fumes will drift into the playground.

However I think the main point is the road will be busy and children will be in danger.

After considering all the evidence and points of view I think it is a bad idea

A completed writing frame

Wray & Lewis (1997) have also developed the idea of writing frames to support children's non-fiction writing. These simply give the basic structure for a piece of writing by setting out a sequence of cohesive ties into which the writer can then enter appropriate content.

This strategy has proved especially useful for children with reading problems, many of whom have managed through it to produce the most logically ordered and well-written pieces of information writing of their lives. An example of a completed writing frame appears on the page opposite and more can be found in Lewis & Wray (1996).

> See *Resource sheets* for examples of writing frames which can be used to scaffold various types of non-fiction writing.

What do children need to know?

> Knowing about language and knowing how to use language

Clearly, considerations about how children learn and the implications of these for approaches to teaching are only part of the story. We also need to have a clear view of what it is that children are to learn in English before we can sensibly plan a teaching programme. The National Curriculum for English gives a progressive description of this learning and the Framework of Teaching Objectives introduced as part of the National Literacy Project and Strategy amplifies this description. There are two main parts to this description: children's knowledge about language and its application in reading and writing, and their skills in applying this knowledge.

Language and literacy knowledge

This knowledge has a number of components that are essential if the child is to be a successful reader, writer, speaker and listener. These include knowledge of the English language and its components and knowledge of a variety of socially important texts.

> The research which led up to the compilation of this review of literacy knowledge was funded by the Teacher Training Agency and is more fully reported in Medwell, J. & Wray, D. (1998) *Effective Teachers of Literacy*, Teacher Training Agency.

Linguistic and metalinguistic knowledge

There are a number of ways to describe the English language: the model which underpins the National Curriculum for English was developed in the Kingman report (DES, 1988). The various elements of linguistic knowledge that children need in order to be literate include elements such as letter recognition, sound-symbol correspondence and grammatical conventions. They also include knowledge about how these elements operate within the English language and the importance of this metalinguistic knowledge has been stressed by a number of researchers (e.g. Downing & Valtin, 1984). In order to become fully literate children need both knowledge of language (how to use it), and knowledge about language (how it is structured).

This knowledge can be summarized at a number of levels: word and sub-word level (phonics, spelling and vocabulary); sentence level (grammar and punctuation); text level (features of texts and genres). At each of these levels, a more detailed list of knowledge components can be outlined.

Word and sub-word level
- Phonological and alphabetical knowledge
  e.g. letter shape recognition, knowing that words are built up from

letters and letter groups with sound values, the ability to recognize rhyme and analyse spoken language

- Knowledge of spelling strings and patterns
  e.g. knowing the patterned basis to spelling (there are a limited number of possible spellings for individual syllables), understanding the role of morphemes in spelling (-ed, -ing, sub-, pre-, etc.)

- Vocabulary knowledge
  e.g. word origins, extended vocabulary, synonyms, antonyms, homonyms and homophones

Sentence level
- Grammatical knowledge
  e.g. knowing word classes (i.e. nouns, verbs, adjectives), grammatical functions in sentences (i.e. subject, verb, object), syntax (i.e. word order and the relationship between words in sentences)

- Punctuation knowledge
  e.g. knowing the uses of a range of punctuation marks and the ways these function as meaning markers in written texts

Text level
- Knowledge of text structures
  e.g. knowing that types of texts (e.g. stories, arguments, explanations and instructions) are structured differently and understanding the structural differences between types of texts

- Knowledge of text features
  e.g. knowing about plot, events and characters in stories

Text knowledge
A further area of knowledge for children is their awareness and knowledge of socially important texts. This includes knowledge of the accepted canon of literature, suitable for their ages, which would allow them to play an appropriate role in an educated society. Children also need to know the conventions of accessing texts in the contemporary world, including book handling and the use of computers and other information sources.

Language and literacy skills

Knowledge of and about the English language is a necessary, but not a sufficient, condition to ensure effective language use. Such use would be more completely defined as the ability to use language knowledge effectively, that is, as a group of linked competencies. Moreover, it is necessary for children to be able to vary their use of these competencies to fit their immediate context. This flexible use of language skills and knowledge separates the effective language user from the ineffective.

The skills of literacy necessarily include the ability to use the knowledge specified above at the word, sentence and text levels. Children need, for example, to be able to use phonic, graphic, syntactic and contextual information to read words and sentences. They need also to use their knowledge of words, spelling patterns and grammatical sequences to write coherently. Their skills must also include all levels of comprehension and composition.

Comprehension includes:

- the ability to understand words and other meaningful units of text on a literal level

- the ability to use a range of strategies to identify the meanings of words

- the ability to go beyond the text by making inferences based on the text and knowledge of the wider world

- the ability to interrogate the text for specific items of information

- the ability to compare and appreciate texts.

Composition of texts depends on a wide range of skills, including:

- letter formation and handwriting skills

- spelling skills

- the ability to create appropriate sentences

- the identification of an audience, purpose and aim for a piece of writing

- the use of the conventions of a genre to shape writing effectively

- the ability to plan, revise, redraft and edit writing.

The use of comprehension and composition skills involves children in a further level of metalinguistic awareness. Literacy users must understand the purposes and functions of literacy activities and have a degree of awareness of the skills they use to achieve these. It is also useful for them to be able to monitor and regulate their comprehension strategies and their composing processes. Studies suggest, for example, that successful readers are aware of when they do not understand what they are reading and can then adopt an appropriate strategy to remedy this situation. Similarly, successful writers are those who have a clear understanding of the writing task (including the demands of its audience) and create mental structures which monitor their writing against their intentions. As with knowledge about language, it is useful for children and teachers to have a shared vocabulary about the skills involved in literacy, so that they can be discussed as part of teaching and learning.

Finally, to be an effective language user, it is not enough to learn the appropriate skills and knowledge without being able to use them flexibly in a range of contexts, both in and out of school. As with all learning, the transfer of language skills from the context in which they were learnt to contexts in which they are useful is problematic. For this reason children must use skills such as reading and writing for a range of purposes and audiences rather than learn simply to read and write in decontextualized situations such as exercises.

Beginning teachers and teaching English

The ITT National Curriculum for primary English specifies the essential core of knowledge, understanding and skills which all emerging primary teachers must be able to use. It is structured in three sections, as follows:

Section A sets out what trainee teachers must be taught during their training courses in order to understand how to develop children's abilities to use English effectively.

Section B sets out the teaching and assessment methods which trainee teachers must be taught and be able to use.

Section C sets out the knowledge and understanding of English which trainee teachers need to underpin their teaching of primary English.

Section C of these requirements, dealing with trainee teachers' knowledge and understanding about English itself, was covered in the companion volume to this, *English for Primary Teachers* (Wray & Medwell, 1997). Sections A and B are more pertinent to the present volume and the requirements they set out are summarized below.

Knowledge and understanding of how to develop pupils' competence in English

The following areas of understanding are demanded by the new requirements.

Teachers need to understand the key aspects of progression in pupils' speaking and listening, reading, writing, spelling and handwriting and also know how to ensure that pupils progress:

- from using implicit knowledge of how language works, to understanding it explicitly so they can evaluate how well they and others speak and write

- from using informal and personal forms of language in both writing and talking, to using more formal and impersonal forms, including standard English

- from a limited awareness of audience, to speech and writing which shows adaptation to different audiences

- from using non-conventional writing, to the use of conventional letter formation, spelling and grammar

- from speaking, reading and writing where fluency is dependent on adult intervention, to independent control of a variety of forms of language.

Teachers also need to understand that pupils' progress in speaking, listening, reading and writing depends on:

- their experience of spoken language in a wide variety of contexts

- their experience of language sounds, structures and patterns in oral language, and later their connection to written text

- their experience of hearing, discussing, retelling and inventing stories and recounting and describing events

- their understanding of how spoken language is related to print, including the understanding of the conventions of writing in English, namely that writing generally progresses from left to right, from top to bottom and from the front to the back of a book.

Also required is an understanding that to read, write and spell individual words, pupils must be taught to:

- hear, identify and synthesize the constituent sounds which make up words, first through onset and rime and then through phonemic segmentation

- recognize and be able to write the letters that represent sounds

- synthesize phonemes into words for reading, and split blends and words into phonemes for spelling

- know that many phonemes have several spellings

- recognize and be able to write an increasingly complex range of phonemes, including digraphs, trigraphs and consonant blends

- recognize patterns of spelling related to word families, letter strings and derivations

- develop and use their aural and visual memory.

Teachers must also be aware that to understand the meaning of individual words, groups of words, sentences and whole texts, pupils must be taught to:

- recognize individual words and groups of words rapidly and automatically

- use known words, syntax and context, as well as information gained from outside the text, to make sense of unknown words and to interpret words where meaning is ambiguous

- interpret the significance of groups of words by recognizing the syntactic boundaries in text, including the use of punctuation to separate clauses and phrases

- combine the meanings of phrases and clauses to gain an understanding of sentences and whole texts

- use phonic, graphic, grammatical and contextual strategies and how to combine them.

Further, teachers must understand that, to extend their reading and their ability to understand the meanings of whole texts, pupils must be taught to:

- recognize and recall material explicitly stated in the text

- make inferences and deductions – drawing conclusions from information which is not explicitly stated in the text

- analyse aspects of the text including argument, structure and plot and use speculation and hypothesis based on their wider reading and previous experience.

Teachers also need to be able to recognize common pupil errors and misconceptions in English and understand how these arise, particularly in such areas as:

- subject/verb agreement

- verb tenses

- the use of apostrophes.

In addition, teachers need to know how to develop and extend pupils' reading and writing and therefore need to know:

- the range, structures and features of novels, plays, poetry, non-fiction and informational texts suitable for use with their pupils

- how to evaluate the quality of these texts

- how to develop pupils' appreciation and evaluation of such texts

- how to evaluate their suitability for different teaching purposes.

Effective teaching methods

Teachers should know that teaching programmes must include time dedicated to the systematic and focused teaching of reading, writing (including spelling and handwriting), speaking and listening. They should also know how to teach the essential core of graphic and phonic knowledge including such aspects as:

- the alphabet and how the letters of the alphabet are used in different combinations to represent the sounds of English

- letter names and sounds and the most common digraphs

- initial and final phonemes

- short-vowel phonemes

- synthesis of phonemes into words for reading and splitting of words into phonemes for spelling

- synthesis of consonant phonemes into consonant blends

- long-vowel phonemes and other common phonemes

- more complex patterns and irregularities

To teach this core, they should be able to use:

- direct instruction and well-paced, interactive oral work

- multi-sensory approaches, including seeing print and hearing it read simultaneously, hearing words or parts of words and writing the corresponding word accurately

- activities and teaching materials which focus directly on the letter pattern being taught including those which involve alliteration, sound patterns and rhymes, and the skilful use of songs, stories, poems and language games.

This concept of text, sentence and word level study is fundamental to the work outlined in the National Literacy Strategy.

They should also be able to teach reading at whole word, sentence and whole text levels through:

- shared reading of texts of high quality with the whole class and with small groups in order to teach reading strategies and model effective reading with larger groups of children, using appropriately differentiated questioning to match individual ability

- guided reading of multiple copies of the same text with groups of children, discussing key features of a text both in advance of and during the reading and structuring and supporting independent silent reading and rereading of the text

- guided silent reading

- focused reading sessions with individual pupils

- reading aloud expressively to the whole class.

Similarly essential is the ability to:

- teach pupils to understand and respond to increasingly challenging and demanding texts

- develop pupils' enthusiasm for reading so that they read independently for pleasure and information

- teach pupils to compare, evaluate and synthesize information from different texts and to locate relevant information quickly through skimming and scanning texts.

Teachers must know how to teach writing, including how to:

- teach spelling to individuals, groups and the whole class

- teach pupils strategies for learning to spell, drawing on their knowledge of sound-symbol relationships, word recognition, word meanings and derivations

- introduce the information contained in different types of dictionaries and its uses

- use a range of teaching and reinforcement approaches, including look-copy-cover-write-check, visual reinforcement, the use of dictionaries, spell checkers, word lists and mnemonics

- teach handwriting so that pupils acquire a fluent, joined and legible style which can be adapted for different purposes

- teach compositional skills through setting clear writing objectives for pupils in terms of features such as content, structure and organization, setting clear criteria for assessment, providing examples drawn from different types of text, teaching and exemplifying each element of the writing process (planning, drafting, revising, editing, proof-reading and presenting), drawing on pupils' knowledge of spoken language and reading as a model or stimulus for writing and for increasing their awareness of differences between spoken and written language

- teach punctuation through direct instruction of rules and conventions of punctuation, as part of the process of writing through proof-reading for example, through activities which include reading aloud so that pupils recognize the role of punctuation in marking grammatical boundaries and in symbolizing the intonation of speech, through marking pupils' written work for punctuation in ways which ensure pupils proof-read and correct their own work independently.

Teachers should also know how to teach speaking and listening through planned activities which require pupils to:

- be articulate and coherent

- adapt their speech for different purposes and situations using different registers as appropriate

- use standard English

- listen attentively

- participate effectively in discussion

- develop and extend their vocabulary.

Methods of assessing progress in English
Teachers should also understand how to assess English, and in particular should know:

See *Monitoring children's progress in primary English* for outlines of a number of approaches to assessing progress.

- how to use diagnostic and summative methods of assessing progress, such as the assessment of pupils' strengths and weaknesses in using language through listening to children talking and reading, observing their writing and analysing the patterns in any strengths and weaknesses shown and the analysis of pupil errors through the use of miscue analysis and running records

- how to make summative assessments of individual pupils' progress and achievement in English through the use of National Curriculum tests, baseline assessment, teacher assessment and other forms of individual pupil assessment, including standardized reading and spelling tests

- how to recognize the standards of attainment they should expect of their pupils in English, taking into account the expected demands in relation to each relevant level description for Key Stage 1 and Key Stage 2 in English

- how to identify under-achieving and very able pupils in English

- how national, local, comparative and school data about achievement in English can be used to identify under-achievement and to set clear expectations and targets

- how inspection and research evidence and international comparisons on the teaching of English can inform teaching.

Teaching episodes examined

Introduction

In this chapter we present three episodes of teaching involving primary English work. The episodes involve the following:

- Key Stage 1 children using reading to learn
- Key Stage 2 children using a shared text as a basis for sentence level work
- Key Stage 2 children involved in a group discussion activity using a text

In each of these episodes we try to pull out the ways in which the key principles for teaching, outlined in the previous chapter, were adapted by the three teachers.

All three teaching episodes show work that was either carried out as part of a literacy hour or could easily have been adapted to fit that mode of classroom organization.

Episode 1: Using non-fiction at Key Stage 1

Classroom context

Year 2 children using non-fiction texts in a meaningful context

Amy, Kelly, Barry, Lisa, Simon, Lorraine and Charlotte are members of a Year 2 class in a school in the south west of England. They work in a pleasant open-plan classroom that borders on a central school courtyard. The class is responsible for the upkeep of the flowerbeds in the courtyard and some of the children attend a weekly after-school gardening club run by parent helpers. It is June and the school has decided to spend some money on hanging baskets containing plants to liven up the courtyard. The children are keen to discuss the contents of these baskets and, because of this keenness, their teacher, Mrs Cox, decides to get them involved in choosing appropriate plants. Later they will visit the local garden centre to purchase their chosen plants but before that the children, in discussion with their teacher, realize that only certain plants will be suitable and that in order to plan successful baskets they will have to do some research.

The work reported here was carried out as part of the Exeter Extending Literacy (EXEL) project. A full account of this project, including the case study referred to in this chapter, can be found in Wray, D. & Lewis, M. (1997) *Extending Literacy*, Routledge.

During this research these children:

- set clear purposes for their work
- drew up a framework for recording information
- located information in a range of reference materials

- collaboratively constructed their understanding of the information they located
- made their recommendations for the purchase of plants
- were empowered by the knowledge they had constructed.

Children as researchers

Structuring the research

The children in this class had a clear purpose to their research. Their teacher, Mrs Cox, had guided them to make the focus as explicit and structured as possible. Simply to ask them to 'find out' about the plants would have been much too vague and vast a task. As the children were relatively inexperienced researchers Mrs Cox had suggested that a grid would help focus their research and provide a scaffold for the kind of questions they might want to ask. Through discussion she was able to draw upon their prior knowledge of gardening, flowers and hanging baskets. As they brainstormed what they already knew she wrote down their comments. Certain themes emerged which they drew together under several headings – height, spread, colour, flowers and leaves, smell. Together they constructed a grid and the children then copied this into their jotters.

> These learning aims might seem ambitious for Year 2 children, but one of the major outcomes of the EXEL project was a realization that it is very easy to underestimate the capabilities of children. Being in a meaningful context enabled these children to achieve more than their teacher thought they were capable of.

NAME OF PLANT	COLOUR	HEIGHT	FRAGRANCE	FOLIAGE	TRAILING?	SPREAD

Notice how the teacher was able to extend their technical vocabulary, substituting 'fragrance' for 'smell' and 'foliage' for 'leaves'. By introducing these words at this stage she was also preparing them for the vocabulary they might encounter when they started to look in books. Because the information the children would need to find would necessarily be quite technical, it quickly became apparent that the reference books already available to the class were largely inadequate in terms of the level of detail they contained. The teacher was able to make available, with the help of the children themselves, several adult gardening books and pamphlets. Many children were so keen that they persuaded their parents to take them to local garden centres and stores to find reference material, much of which they could pick up for no cost. Of course, these materials were designed for adult readers, and their vocabulary, layout and print size made few concessions to infant readers.

Each heading of the grid the children had helped design acted both as a question to be answered and a 'key word' to focus the children's research and perhaps even to help with scanning the text for that particular word.

> The headings targetted the children's reading and made it much less likely that they would simply copy sections from the books.

Classroom talk as evidence of learning

As the children got underway with their research, they naturally talked together about their tasks. Three distinct kinds of talk were used and these can be referred to as modelled talk, collaborative talk and tangential talk. Each of these in their own ways functioned as enablers of children's learning.

Modelled talk

Before they began their enquiries the teacher discussed with the children where they might find the information they needed. The children suggested several sources: books, asking 'experts' (i.e. members of the gardening club), looking at other hanging baskets, asking their parents, watching gardening programmes on television. At this point the teacher modelled for them how they might select and use information books. As she did this she talked about what she was doing and why. She was making what is usually an internal monologue accessible to the children. One extract from her demonstration was as follows:

> *Now which of these books shall I use? This book's got flowers on the cover so it might be useful and the title ... yes,* Garden Flowers, *that tells me it might be useful. Now what do I do? Yes, I can look in the index. Let's look up hanging baskets in the index. So I'm going to turn to the back of the book. Here it is. Index. Now. It's arranged alphabetically a... d... g... h... h... here it is. H. Lets look for ha ...*

Through this kind of modelling she was making explicit to the children the thought processes she was going through and was therefore able to give the children some very important lessons on what it is an experienced reader does. The importance of teachers demonstrating rather than simply telling children about the problem-solving, planning and strategic decision-making which characterize the reading process cannot be over-emphasized. Modelling enables teachers to make explicit the thought processes that accompany involvement in literate activities, processes which, by their very nature, are invisible.

This is an example of the meta-reading which we mentioned in *Learning and teaching literacy.*

There were many subsequent instances of the children apparently using the same kind of externalized thinking to guide their own work. Here, for example, are Amy and Kelly searching for information about nasturtiums.

AMY: This one got anything? (*Picks up a book*).

KELLY: I need to copy. (*Looks at the spelling of nasturtiums in Amy's jotter and writes.*)

AMY: 'Index'. It should be here somewhere. Yes ... right ... what does it say? Nasturtiums ... it hasn't got it there. I'll have to go to the contents. Turn to the front. Ah, here it is. (*Searches contents page. Cannot find desired entry.*) It'll have to be another book. (*Scans pile of books on offer.*)

KELLY: Look in that one. (*Points to book.*)

AMY: Yeah. I'll look in this one. (*Picks up book indicated by Kelly.*)

KELLY: (*Holds front cover with Amy.*) What's it say? (*Reads.*) 'Ornamental Kitchen Garden'.

AMY: This is the one I had. (*Browsing through some pages of pictures, but actively searching.*) This tells us about ... hardy petunias ... French marigolds ... nasturtiums? ... sweet williams ... Lizzie busies ... Lizzie busies. Midsummer Plants. (*Reading page heading.*) 'Marigolds'. I've got some of those in my back yard. (*Muttered conversation between the two while they keep on 'browse searching'.*) Where's it gone? Nasturtium.

KELLY: Have a look in another book. (*Amy and Kelly each pick up another book.*) Have a look in the index.

AMY: Index. Right. (*Both looking in index of their book.*) Nasturtiums ... nasturtiums. GOT IT. 157... 157... 157. (*Turning pages and checking number.*) Here. Nasturtiums.

Should be here somewhere. (*Scanning page.*) There it is. Height 1 foot ... 30cms. Well done. I found it. (*Kelly begins to write. Amy closes book.*) I don't know the colour yet, do I? (*Colour is the next column on the grid. Reopens book.*) 157 ... Right ... What's the colour? What's the colour? (*Reads aloud.*) Red, orange, yellow. Red, orange, yellow. We'd better get red. (*Closes book again.*)

KELLY: How do you spell ...? (*Both write in colour column.*)

AMY: (*Looking at grid.*) Right. Fragrance. What's its fragrance? Has it got a fragrance or has it not? I don't think ... (*Opens book and searches for page 157 again.*) Now where's it gone?

The children are going through the process of hunting for particular information but they are continually 'talking themselves through' this process. It is noticeable that the language they use is very close to that which was previously modelled to them by their teacher. Amy's 'Nasturtiums ... it hasn't got it there. I'll have to go to the contents. Turn to the front. Ah, here it is', for example, might almost have come directly from the demonstration they received earlier from their teacher.

Kelly's role in this extract also seems to be derived from the talk she has witnessed her teacher using. She continually prompts Amy to carry out particular actions: 'Look in that one', 'Have a look in another book', 'Have a look in the index'. These are exactly the kinds of directions her teacher will undoubtedly have given many times in the past. Both Amy and Kelly are using talk to guide their actions and they have learnt to do this by listening to the talk used by their teacher.

- -

Social learning as shown through collaborative talk

Collaborative talk

The social, interactive nature of the task was important. On numerous occasions the children prompted each other to continue working, to try another technique if they could not find what they were looking for, discussed information, worked together to try to understand difficult text and asked each other for help and advice. Here, for example, are Amy and Kelly again, this time searching for information about the plant known as Busy Lizzie (its Latin name is *Impatiens*).

KELLY: Let's look in the index. Where did it say Busy Lizzie? (*Both looking.*)

AMY: Busy Lizzie. I'll look in another book. (*Kelly continues scanning original index.*)

KELLY: Oh why? So that's ... 48. (*Starts to turn to page 48. Notices a picture.*) Oh look. Mrs Henry Cox. (*Amy glances at picture.*) Mrs Cox is a flower. (*Amy looks again. Both laugh.*)

AMY: Where? (*Kelly points. Both laugh.*)

KELLY: There. It says Mrs Henry Cox.

AMY: Yes ... but we're not looking for that, are we? We're trying to look for Busy Lizzie.

KELLY: I've got Busy Lizzies.

AMY: I know.

KELLY: (*Turning pages*) 48 ... Busy Lizzie ... page 48 ... way past that ... page 48. (*Arrives, scans it. Amy gets up and looks over Kelly's shoulder.*)

AMY: I'll look for it. (*Starts looking in another book.*) I'll look for it. Don't you worry, Kelly, I'm good at looking in books. Busy Lizzie ... 100 ... 150 ... (*finds page 150*). That's where it is. Should be here somewhere. (*Closes book when fails to find it.*) Right ... I'll try ... this one. (*Takes another book.*) Now what? (*Turns to index, scanning*) ... 83 (*Turns to page 83.*) ... Busy Lizzie. (*Finds and reads text aloud to herself.*) That's not very much. (*Closes book.*) I hate this, I'm never going to find things. Right. Now what? I'm still ...

KELLY: They're going to assembly. (*Amy turns and looks.*) They've got to, haven't they? (*Amy doesn't respond. Both girls pick up book and again turn to index.*)

AMY: Busy Lizzie ... see ... emporer ... What? ... Busy Lizzie ... What? Busy Lizzie, see emporer or something. What? Weird! (*Kelly glances across.*) See impoorer. What? ... This, see. This one says Busy Lizzie see imp ... emporer ... or something.

KELLY: What are we looking for then?

AMY: Busy Lizzies. (*Both look at Amy's book.*)

KELLY: That's strange. I'm telling Miss. (*Both leave table.*)

There is clear collaboration here from both girls even though Amy takes the dominant role. This is a shared activity and the girls are co-constructing their own ways through it. It is also interesting that they are able to share a (gentle) joke at the expense of their teacher when they discover a flower with the same name but bring themselves rapidly back to the task.

> This is shared consciousness in action. The girls were enabling each other to think at a higher level than they could achieve individually.

The problem that bothered Amy towards the end of this extract was discovering in the index of her book the entry 'Busy Lizzie. See *Impatiens*'. The girls eventually took this to their teacher who had to explain to them the conventions of cross-referencing and the use of Latin plant names. Amy and Kelly simply listened to this explanation and carried on with their work. This incident provides some good evidence of the power of authentic activities. It is unlikely that the teacher here would have planned to introduce six-year-olds to cross-referencing or Latin plant names, yet in the context in which the girls are working this apparently complex information causes them very little difficulty.

Of course, collaboration was not always as unproblematic as this. The natural egocentricity of six-year-old children occasionally got in the way. In the following extract, for example, Lisa and Barry have some problems with collaboration although they do eventually resolve them.

TEACHER: (*to Lisa*) Do you know what a fuchsia is?

BARRY: (*who is a member of the gardening club, interrupts and is ignored*) Yes. We've got them in the garden.

TEACHER: (*to Lisa*) Do you know what colour it is? Have a look in the index.

BARRY: Yes. We've got one in the garden (*pointing*).

TEACHER: (*to Lisa*) You can look up fuchsia in the index or you can talk to Barry about it. He seems to know a lot about it. (*Teacher leaves*).

BARRY: (*to Lisa*) You can look over there. We've got one over there. I've seen it thousands of times.

LISA: (*Searching for a particular page in a book, having looked in the index.*) Is that it there? (*Shows him a picture. They both look.*)

BARRY: What? In there? ... Do you want to look out of the window and I'll show you?

LISA: (*with mock reluctance, getting up*) Oh ... (*Both go to the window.*)

BARRY: (*pointing*) That one there. See that one there. (*Lisa nods.*)

The children remained at the window for about a minute and were joined by another child who also wanted to look before being ushered back to their seats by a passing adult. On her way back to the table Lisa remarked to Barry that the fuchsias in the garden were a different colour from the one in the picture in the book. She later recorded this on her grid, where she wrote 'purple and pink or they can be white'.

In this brief incident we see Barry clearly determined to display his expertise and able to use his past experience and the availability of real examples to share his knowledge with his peers. Lisa was initially reluctant to be distracted from her task of finding information in a book but eventually relented and went along with Barry's alternative strategy. In doing this she learnt something about using different sources of information and also that these do not always agree. Both children were learning to be critical of texts they read.

> Critical reading is an essential aspect of literacy to which children are rarely introduced.

Tangential talk

Anecdotes in learning

There were plenty of examples, of course, of children talking together in a way which might simply be seen as conversation which had little to do with the task in which they were engaged. Such talk can be referred to as tangential although this should not be taken to mean irrelevant. In fact, much of this conversation did originate from the task itself and in itself it can often function as a prime mechanism for learning. In the following extract, for example, Barry was searching for a picture of a marigold when a quite different picture caught his attention.

BARRY: Oh! look at that ... that's ... that's ... It's made out of flowers. (*Points to picture of a flower bed laid out as a ship.*)

LISA: There's a Mickey Mouse one ... other ones in other places.

BARRY: Woah! That's brilliant.

LISA: I've seen them millions of times.

BARRY: (*to Simon*) Have you seen them at Torquay? They've got them. Made out of flowers. Them.

SIMON: Where?

BARRY: Torquay. Where they make them models out of flowers. You been to Torquay? (*Simon shakes his head*). Been to Paignton?

LISA: I've been to Paignton.

A teacher arriving at this moment might be tempted to conclude that the children were not on task but in some ways they certainly were, being involved in making their own connections with the material they were working with. This linking of previous knowledge and experience to new material is a crucial part of the researching and learning process and reaffirms the importance of conversation rather than silence in young children's learning through inquiry

> We all engage in this kind of talk, making links between new knowledge and old by telling stories, or anecdotes, about our previous experience.

Information is power.

Empowerment through information

Two of the children had a very important lesson that morning. Lorraine and Charlotte learnt that information can be empowering.

The pair had begun by browsing through the gardening books, looking at pictures. From these pictures they decided that they wanted their hanging baskets to contain tomatoes, strawberries and a bonsai tree. They wrote the names of these three plants into the first column of their grid and were about to start looking for further information when their teacher joined them. She pointed out that their suggestions were unusual and that they would need to find some good evidence to support these choices. Charlotte and Lorraine were not deflected from their ideas and started to research. In one gardening book they discovered a variety of dwarf trailing tomatoes. In another they found a picture of strawberries in a planter which clearly suggested that these were trailing plants. They presented these findings to their teacher, who was clearly a little flustered and could only respond, 'But bonsai trees don't grow in baskets. I think you should check that one carefully!'

The children turned their attention to bonsai trees. They discovered a section in one book on the growing and training of bonsai trees. This gave them the information that bonsai trees 'can be trained into any shape'. They reasoned from this that they could train their bonsai tree to trail over their basket. They worked out that they would need wire for this task but they did fail to realize that it might take them 50 years to grow their tree! When their teacher returned they were ready to argue their case and defend their choice of plants.

What these children had learnt was that, armed with the appropriate information, you can argue with powerful and important people such as your teacher. Knowledge can give you the power to argue your case – a lesson central to democracy. Their teacher was humane and responsive enough to concede the argument, not wishing at this point to dampen the children's enthusiasm. It should be noted, however, that when it came to trying to convince their classmates, Lorraine and Charlotte had a much more difficult task!

Applying teaching principles

Conclusion

The children involved in this teaching episode were learning a number of things. You should have already noticed how the teacher was able to use the principles for teaching outlined earlier. This can be summarized as follows:

Building upon learners' previous knowledge
The experiences the children underwent were very dependent upon them having sufficient existing knowledge about plants and flowers and the teacher made specific mention of their experiences in gardening clubs and of flowers they grew at home.

Making provision for group interaction and discussion
The children were deliberately placed in groups to work and their recommendations for plants to grow were the result of group deliberations. The social nature of the activity was fundamental to its success and to the children's learning, as shown by several of the talk extracts given above.

Ensuring meaningful contexts for learning
The children were learning in a context where the outcomes mattered to them and the skills they were practising were being put immediately to use.

Promoting learners' knowledge and awareness of their own thinking and learning
By modelling ways of thinking and reading the teacher was making the children more explicitly aware of these processes.

Episode 2: Working with fiction at Key Stage 2

Teaching through a shared text

Classroom context

This Year 3 class was studying an extract from Dick King Smith's book *The Hodgeheg*. The extract was part of the first page of the story. It starts:

"Your Auntie Betty has copped it," said Pa Hedgehog to Ma.

"Oh no!" cried Ma. "Where?"

"Just down the road. Opposite the newsagent's. Bad place to cross, that."

"Everywhere's a bad place to cross nowadays," said Ma. "The traffic's dreadful. Do you realize, Pa, that's the third this year, and all on my side of the family too. First there was Grandfather, then my second cousin once removed and now poor old Auntie Betty ...".

They were sitting in a flower bed at their home, the garden of Number 5A of a row of semi-detached houses in a suburban street. On the other side of the road was a park, very popular with the local hedgehogs on account of the good hunting it offered. As well as worms and slugs and snails, which they could find in their own gardens, there were special attractions in the park. Mice lived under the bandstand, feasting on the crumbs dropped from listeners' sandwiches; frogs dwelt in the lily pond and in the ornamental gardens grass-snakes slithered through the shrubbery. All these creatures were regarded as great delicacies by the hedgehogs, and they could never resist the occasional night's sport in the park. But to reach it, they had to cross the busy road.

The aims of this lesson were twofold:

- to remind children of the key features of a narrative opening – the opening paragraph, the setting, characters and plot
- to examine the conventions of direct speech.

This lesson was the second time the teacher had used the passage for shared reading. The previous day the literacy hour had involved this passage and a discussion of its meaning and content.

> It is important when using shared reading like this that you return to texts, sometimes several times. Children's understanding of the texts will be extended with each fresh look.

Shared reading

Mrs Hall put a transparency of the opening passage from the book on to the overhead projector so that all the children could see it projected on to the wall. Some children also had photocopied sheets of the passage. The lesson began with Mrs Hall telling the children, 'We are going to read this piece again and pick out some of the features of the beginning of a story. There are some things which are important about stories and I want you to use them when you write yours.'

> The use of the overhead projector was important here. It is an excellent vehicle for sharing texts with children. Several of the lesson plans given later could involve the use of the OHP.

Mrs Hall asked all the children to read the passage silently to themselves. She then asked them 'Do you remember this from before? Who will start by reading the first sentence?' Mrs Hall picked children to read parts of the passage, from a sentence to a paragraph. When children got stuck on a word, other children supplied words and Mrs Hall asked them, 'How did you know that's what it was?'

Mrs Hall then started to question the class. The question 'How do you know this is a story?' elicited a range of answers, including:
> 'It says Chapter 1.'
> 'The way it says what happened.'
> 'Where it says they were sitting.'
> 'The hedgehogs can't really talk.'
> 'It sounds like a story and you just sort of know.'

Mrs Hall did not comment on all the answers, but made a list on the board of the following:
> hedgehogs talk
> sounds like a story
> tells you what has happened
> tells us where it happened

She told the class that there were some good points in the list and she underlined the points hedgehogs talk, tells us where it happened and sounds like a story. She told the class that these were points they were going to talk about.

She went on to ask them, 'First of all, what about the hedgehogs. They are characters. What does that mean?'

From discussion with the children Mrs Hall established that the characters of a story play a part in what happens in the story. She then asked them how the reader knows what the characters do. The answers given included:
> 'They do things and the story tells you what.'
> 'They say things.'
> 'Other characters tell us about them.'

'Who are the characters in this story?'

In response to children's answers Mrs Hall marked Ma and Pa on the OHP with a pen and asked, 'What do we know about these characters?'

The class volunteered the following information:
> 'Ma and Pa are hedgehogs, so we know what they look like and that they wake up at night.'
> 'They are called Ma and Pa so they are part of a family'
> 'The passage says that they eat slugs and snails and like snakes and crumbs. They are talking about the cars, which are a problem.'
> 'They are nice [sympathetic] characters.'

Mrs Hall returned to the list on the board. 'This is a story because it tells us where it happened.' She tells the class that this is called the story setting.

'Where is the setting for this story?'

The children's answers included the flower bed, the garden of a row of houses and the park. Mrs Hall underlined the sentence which mentioned the flower bed and the row of houses and asked children to volunteer information about 'semi-detached' and 'suburban'. There was some discussion about what the houses might be like. The class also talked about the park. Why was there so much information about the park? Was the park going to be important in the story?

Mrs Hall then turned to time. 'The story begins in the flower bed, but when do you think it happens? After all, to imagine the story properly we need to know where and when to think about.' The class discussed the night-time habits of hedgehogs and how Auntie Betty might have been run over. The consensus was that it must be early in the morning and Betty was run over the night before.

Mrs Hall then asked, 'But is this a modern story or about a long time ago?' The answers were rather slow in coming but finally some children picked out that if Auntie Betty had been run over then there must have been cars. Traffic was mentioned in the text and suburban semi-detached houses were modern.

Mrs Hall raised a new point. 'What will happen next, then? What is the plot of the story?'

> Notice the way the teacher was able to draw upon children's previous knowledge of these features of stories and then to extend them.

The children made predictions – some were little more than guesses but Mrs Hall responded by asking why the child had said that. The 'clue' was the last line of the extract, which mentioned the road, and most of the children agreed that the hedgehogs needed to find a way to cross it safely.

Sentence level work

Mrs Hall moved on to the issue of direct speech by asking who had spoken in this passage. The children easily picked out Ma and Pa Hedgehog and could tell Mrs Hall what they had said. She responded by drawing two bundles of spikes (hedgehogs!) on the board with speech bubbles coming from them and asking the children to tell her what to put in these speech bubbles. 'What was the first thing each character said?' She repeated this for the next piece of direct speech then turned to the class and said, 'It takes so long to draw the speech bubbles. How do we show exactly what someone says in writing?'

> Sentence level work does not necessarily have to focus on a text also used for shared reading, but this episode shows very well the power of doing it this way. The children's learning is contextualized by the text they have worked with.

Focusing on speech marks

The children responded with replies about speech marks. Mrs Hall marked these on the passage and then asked the children about the conventions of punctuation. 'Where do the full stops go?'

To conclude this section, Mrs Hall wrote an imaginary dialogue between herself and Miss Bull (the head) on the board and asked the children to tell her where to add speech marks and start new lines.

> *Good morning said Mrs Hall. Hi said Miss Bull. Outdoor play today groaned Mrs Hall. I'm afraid so said Miss Bull.*

Mrs Hall then introduced a task that the whole class would be doing this week – writing a dialogue between two characters from the class novel *The Owl Who Was Afraid of the Dark*. Mrs Hall discussed which characters might be used and what they might say.

Moving to guided writing

Group and individual tasks

After the whole class work, Mrs Hall gave tasks to the groups. Two groups were asked to complete a photocopied chart of the characters, settings (when and where) and plot of four books. Two were named books that the class had read together and the children were allowed to choose two other books they had read (a blank copy of this chart appears on p.159). One group of children read with the classroom assistant and the other two groups worked with Mrs Hall to write a dialogue between two characters from the class novel. Mrs Hall introduced this task by checking that all the children remembered the concept of dialogue and how this is shown in stories.

Applying teaching principles

Conclusion

The children involved in this teaching episode were learning a number of things. You should have already noticed how the teacher was able to use the principles for teaching outlined earlier. This can be summarized as follows:

Building upon learners' previous knowledge
The children had already been introduced to the particular text they were studying so the content was familiar. The teacher also constantly asked them to recall what they already knew about the key concepts she was teaching – settings and plot, and direct speech. She was able to help them extend this previous knowledge by applying it to a new context.

Making provision for group interaction and discussion
The children were working in a social situation. The whole class was involved in interactive discussion during the shared reading period and Mrs Hall several times reflected a child's comments back to the class as a topic for consideration. This not only helped them to learn through the use of talk, it also indicated that Mrs Hall esteemed the contributions that children were able to make.

During the group work section of the lesson, tasks were deliberately engineered so that children had to collaborate and discuss what they were doing.

Ensuring meaningful contexts for learning
The children were learning some technical features of how texts work within the meaningful context of having experienced an interesting story extract. The text gave the context for the remainder of the children's work.

Promoting learners' knowledge and awareness of their own thinking and learning
By modelling ways of thinking, reading and questioning the teacher was making the children more explicitly aware of these processes. She was also constantly asking them to make explicit the thinking they were engaged in with the text.

Episode 3: A focus on talk

Talking around a text

Classroom context

Jamie, Claire, Michael and Amy are Year 5 children who are used to working together as a group. They are working together on this occasion as part of the independent/group work section of a literacy hour. Their teacher has given them an extract from *Tom Sawyer* to work with and previously she has cut up this extract into paragraphs. The children have been given the paragraphs in a jumbled-up order and their task is to arrange them into an order that makes sense. This sequencing activity is one they are familiar with. They are also familiar with the story of *Tom Sawyer*, as extracts from this have previously been read to them.

This group sequencing activity is just one of a group of activities generally referred to as DARTs – Directed Activities Related to Texts. These include group cloze, prediction and text restructuring. Some of the lesson plans given later suggest some further DARTs work.

The nature of the task

The task the children have been given involves them in some collaborative problem solving, as it is not entirely obvious which order the paragraphs should be in. There are several alternative possibilities for a sequence and the children know that they can choose an order which is different from that originally written by the author, as long as they can justify this order to each other and to their teacher.

The clues available to them to determine an appropriate sequence include the following:
- the likely sequence of events in the extract
- the introduction of characters and descriptions of these characters
- the use of cohesive ties such as pronouns
- particular connectives indicating a time sequence, e.g. first, next, after that
- the settings for the action and the change of these settings

The full text of the extract they were discussing is given below – with paragraphs in the order in which they were presented.

A *A measured, muffled snore issued from Aunt Polly's chamber. And now the tiresome chirping of a cricket that no human ingenuity could locate, began. Next the ghastly ticking of a death-watch in the wall at the bed's head made Tom shudder – it meant that somebody's days were numbered.*

B *By and by, out of the stillness, little, scarcely perceptible noises began to emphasize themselves. The ticking of the clock began to bring itself into notice. Old beams began to crack mysteriously. The stairs creaked faintly. Evidently spirits were abroad.*

C *It was a graveyard of the old-fashioned Western kind. It was on a hill, about a mile and a half from the village. It had a crazy board fence around it, which leaned inward in places, and outward the rest of the time, but stood upright nowhere. Grass and weeds grew rank over the whole cemetery.*

D *At half-past nine, that night, Tom and Sid were sent to bed, as usual. They said their prayers, and Sid was soon asleep. Tom lay awake and waited, in restless impatience. When it seemed to him that it must be nearly daylight, he heard the clock strike ten! This was despair.*

E *They found the sharp new heap they were seeking, and ensconced themselves within the protection of three great elms that grew in a bunch within a few feet of the grave.*

F *Then the howl of a far-off dog rose on the night air, and was answered by a fainter howl from a remoter distance. Tom was in an agony. At last he was satisfied that time had ceased and eternity begun; he began to doze, in spite of himself; the clock chimed eleven, but he did not hear it.*

G *He "meow'd" with caution once or twice, as he went; then jumped to the roof of the woodshed and thence to the ground. Huckleberry Finn was there, with his dead cat. The boys moved off and disappeared in the gloom. At the end of half an hour they were wading through the tall grass of the graveyard.*

H *And then there came, mingling with his half-formed dreams, a most melancholy caterwauling. The raising of a neighboring window disturbed him. A cry of "Scat! You devil!" and the crash of an empty bottle against the back of his aunt's woodshed brought him wide awake, and a single minute later he was dressed and out of the window and creeping along the roof of the "ell" on all fours.*

I *A faint wind moaned through the trees, and Tom feared it might be the spirits of the dead, complaining at being disturbed. The boys talked little, and only under their breath, for the time and the place and the pervading solemnity and silence oppressed their spirits.*

J *All the old graves were sunken in, there was not a tombstone on the place; round-topped, worm-eaten boards staggered over the graves, leaning for support and finding none. "Sacred to the memory of So-and-So" had been painted on them once, but it could no longer have been read, on the most of them, now, even if there had been light.*

K *He would have tossed and fidgeted, as his nerves demanded, but he was afraid he might wake Sid. So he lay still, and stared up into the dark. Everything was dismally still.*

Beginning the activity

As the children got underway with the activity, their group talk was firstly characterized by a good deal of procedural discussion; that is, they talked about how they would carry out the task, who would do what and generally how they would work. The following extract from their talk shows this procedural discussion in action.

AMY: This looks hard. We'd better read them all first.
JAMIE: Yeah. I think I've got the first one. Look, it says 'Tom and Sid were sent to bed'.
MICHAEL: This one says they were in the graveyard. That could have been before they went to bed.
AMY: I think we've got to read them all first.
JAMIE: Yeah. Let's all take a few each to read.
MICHAEL: Hang on. I can't read this ... 'cat ... cat ...' something.
CLAIRE: I've got a 'death watch'. What's that?

Following this initial burst of talk, the children were quiet for a time as they each read to themselves the various paragraphs of the text.

During the remainder of the activity, the group used several kinds of talk.

A range of types of talk

Thinking aloud

The talk of the group was characterized by its tentativeness. Children would often venture suggestions about the likely order of the passage in a way that made it clear these were offered as possibilities rather than firm conclusions. Thus, in talking this way, they were externalizing what they were currently thinking.

An example of this can be seen in Jamie's contribution:

AMY: Who's got one about the graveyard?

JAMIE: I think I have. It says, 'a faint wind moaned through the trees'. That could have been in a graveyard, or somewhere outside. I don't think it was in the bedroom. No, 'cos look, they're talking to each other. I thought Sid was asleep.

Later, Jamie ventured:

JAMIE: It must have been Huckleberry who made the noise. He's here, look, with his dead cat. Why was it dead? The bottle might have killed it?

MICHAEL: Huckleberry had a dead cat, don't you remember from the story? He just used to keep it.

JAMIE: Oh yeah. So he must have had it with him all the time.

Jamie here is thinking through possibilities, aided by the other children who remind him of details that inform his thinking.

Such exposure of their thought processes would only have been possible in a group used to working with one another and who were confident that their suggestions would be taken seriously by the other members of the group.

> One of the findings of research into classroom talk has been that children rarely get the opportunity to ask questions in the way that Jamie does in the second extract. The person in the classroom who asks the most questions is the teacher!

Collaborative thinking

Thinking aloud was not simply an individual thing. Several times members of the group arrived at new ideas through their collaborative talk, ideas which probably they would not have reached individually.

An example of such collaborative thinking can be seen in the following extract.

CLAIRE: Tom's laying in bed in K and keeping quiet. But there are all these noises. The ticking of the clock, the stairs. Are those in the bedroom?

AMY: I think so 'cos it says 'by and by ...'

CLAIRE: Yeah, 'Out of the stillness ...' So he was only hearing those noises 'cos it was so still.

AMY: And when he was really quiet he could hear new things.

Again the presence of such talk demands a high level of trust among the group members. It also depends on a willingness to change your mind and offer up ideas as provisional.

Informative talk

A more straightforward kind of talk, very noticeable in this discussion, was the giving of information to other members of the group. This was sometimes a matter of individuals informing their colleagues of what was in a section of the text that had been overlooked.

CLAIRE: No, he can't be in the graveyard with Sid because it says here, look, 'Huckleberry Finn was there with his dead cat'.

Sometimes children also informed each other of items they knew about from outside the current text.

JAMIE: I think he must have been scared. Sometimes I can hear noises when I'm in bed and it's scary.

MICHAEL: You get scared in bed?!

JAMIE: Yeah. You know, when the floor creaks and our heating starts up.

The regular use of talk to give information in this way again depends upon the children in the group accepting the possibility that others will listen and take notice of what they have to say.

Judgemental talk

When children offered information or suggested lines of thinking, these were often followed by other children offering judgements on these contributions. A good example of this occurred when Michael misunderstood the story.

MICHAEL: It says, 'They found the new heap they were seeking, and en … ens … something, themselves', so Tom and Sid must have been waiting in the graveyard.

AMY: It wasn't Sid.

CLAIRE: No, it can't be Sid. He was asleep. Look, 'Sid was soon asleep'.

The use of this kind of judgemental talk is another indication of the collaborative thinking the children were engaging in. Offering up ideas for them to be evaluated, modified and extended by their colleagues was characteristic of the discussion.

> Of course, judgemental talk can sometimes simply be criticizing. It says a lot for the working relationships of a group if they can go beyond this to use judgements about each others' ideas positively.

Reading and rereading

A very prominent form of talk in this discussion, as you might expect, was the children's reading aloud of extracts from the text they were working on. Sometimes different children would read an extract out several times. Often the meanings attached to the text by the children would only be apparent from the intonation with which they were read. Sometimes, for example, words were emphasized as they were being produced as evidence for a particular line of thought, and sometimes they were read in a questioning tone as the reader asked for clarification of their meaning.

> Rereadings were not simply repeats of what had already been said. They offered evidence of thinking on the part of the children.

Talk as learning

As the children participated in this group discussion, it was clear that they were both learning from and teaching each other. Often, as we have illustrated already, ideas advanced by individuals would be taken up by others, with modifications, extensions or corrections. Thus the thinking of the group was a social enterprise and the talk was an essential vehicle for this.

Reflecting on the experience

During the plenary section of the literacy hour, the group's teacher asked them to explain what they had been doing to their classmates and to say what they thought they had been learning. Naturally the children had a variety of views about this but they were all agreed that they had enjoyed the experience of working together in this way.

Having this opportunity to reflect on what they had been doing, and in particular having to articulate their reflections, caused the children to sharpen their awareness of several things:

- their own thinking
- their ways of relating to colleagues
- approaches to reading
- the role of talk.

Thus the reflection was itself an important part of these children's learning.

> We rarely ask children to reflect upon their own learning. This is a very important way of learning. One major function of the plenary section of the literacy hour is to enable it to happen.

Conclusion

During this activity the children were learning a number of things. Their teacher was also able to use the principles for teaching outlined earlier, although in this case she was not actually present as they undertook the activity. A brief summary of how these principles operated is as follows:

Building upon learners' previous knowledge

The text the children were working with, while not itself one they had previously encountered, did come from a book whose general storyline they were familiar with. They were able to draw upon this previous knowledge of the characters, settings and plots of the book in order to solve the particular problems they were faced with.

They also on occasions drew upon their previous experience outside school to interpret the ideas in the text.

Making provision for group interaction and discussion

The activity depended upon group discussion and we have pointed out above several ways in which this functioned in the children's learning.

Ensuring meaningful contexts for learning

The activity they were engaged in involved the reconstruction of meaning. It was therefore a meaningful context by its very nature and the children treated it as such.

Promoting learners' knowledge and awareness of their own thinking and learning

The activity itself forced children to offer up their ideas to the rest of the group. The feedback they received made them reconsider these ideas and thus reflected their thinking back on itself.

They were also encouraged to reflect upon their thinking in the plenary session and this raised their awareness of their approaches to problems and to reading a text.

Applying teaching principles

The literacy hour

A central part of recent developments in the teaching of literacy is the concept of the literacy hour. This provides a coherent and practical structure to the teaching of literacy and has a number of benefits, which will be discussed below.

The literacy hour is structured into four main sections:

Shared text work, with a focus on text level study
This consists of approximately 15 minutes whole class work using a text such as a Big Book, or a piece of writing the class are composing together. It may involve shared reading, during which the teacher supports the class in reading and understanding a text that would probably be beyond their individual capabilities. Such shared reading also provides the context for introducing word and sentence level features such as phonics and grammar within a context of meaningful interaction with a text. This section may also involve shared writing in which, through the collaborative composition of a text, the teacher can support the class in such processes as drafting, revising, editing and proof-reading.

Focused word or sentence level work
With Key Stage 1 children this 10–15 minute section provides the opportunity for the systematic teaching of phonological awareness, phonic knowledge and spelling. There needs to be a progressive programme of such work, although in ideal circumstances it can be linked into the text used earlier in the literacy hour. With Key Stage 2 children this section should be focused on the teaching of sentence level work such as grammar and punctuation, as well as word level work such as vocabulary extension and spelling. Again a systematic programme is needed although often this work can be drawn naturally from the shared text.

Independent or group work on a range of literacy activities
This consists of 20–30 minutes of activities planned to fit with the overall programme in the class. During this time the teacher should aim to work with one or two groups using guided reading or writing, that is, highly structured sessions in which children read and/or write independently but under the direction of the teacher.

The best information so far published about the literacy hour is in the *National Literacy Strategy Framework for Teaching*, published by the Department for Education and Employment, 1998.

Plenary time
With the whole class, the work accomplished during the literacy hour can be reviewed, evaluated and extended.

We will spend some time later in this chapter exploring in more detail the possibilities of each of these parts of the literacy hour.

The benefits of a literacy hour approach

Why use a literacy hour?

The main benefits of organizing literacy teaching in this way are, according to the National Literacy Strategy:
- an explicit focus on literacy instruction
- improved classroom organization and management
- effective management of literacy at school level

An explicit focus on literacy instruction
The claim of the National Literacy Strategy is that the most successful teaching is:

- discursive – that is, characterized by high-quality discussion and classroom talk and, in particular by the use of searching and stimulating teacher questions

- interactive – pupils are not allowed to remain passive but their contributions are encouraged and extended by the teacher

- well-paced – there is a strong sense of urgency in the teaching and everyone in the classroom is encouraged to keep up a brisk learning pace

- confident – teachers who understand clearly what it is they are teaching are likely to approach it with much greater confidence of success

- ambitious – there are high expectations of children and what they can achieve

> These characteristics of effective literacy teaching were broadly endorsed by the findings of the Effective Teachers of Literacy Project (Medwell & Wray, 1998).

Such teaching is implied in the literacy hour which, because of its tight focus and pace is more likely to engender high levels of motivation and active pupil engagement. A wide range of teaching strategies are recommended, including the following:

Teaching strategies in the literacy hour

- direction – e.g. to ensure pupils know what they should be doing, to draw attention to points, to develop key strategies in reading and writing

- demonstration – e.g. to teach letter formation and how to join letters, how to read punctuation using a shared text, how to use a dictionary

- modelling – e.g. discussing the features of written texts through shared reading of books, extracts, etc.

- scaffolding – e.g. providing writing frames for shared composition of non-fiction texts

- explanation to clarify and discuss – e.g. reasons in relation to the events in a story, the need for grammatical agreement when proof-reading, the way that different kinds of writing are used to serve different purposes

- questioning – to probe pupils' understanding, to cause them to reflect on and refine their work, and to extend their ideas

- initiating and guiding exploration – e.g. to develop phonological awareness in the early stages, to explore relationships between grammar, meaning and spelling with older pupils

- investigating ideas – e.g. to understand, expand on or generalize about themes and structures in fiction and non-fiction

- discussing and arguing – to put points of view, argue a case, justify a preference, etc.

- listening to and responding – e.g. to stimulate and extend pupils' contributions, to discuss/evaluate their presentations.

Improved classroom organization and management

The main aim of the literacy hour is to offer a classroom management structure that maximizes the time teachers spend directly teaching. It shifts the balance of teaching away from individualized work and towards more whole-class and group teaching. There are good reasons for this shift. In the past, where children have been taught individually for much of their school time, the actual teaching time they have experienced has often been limited. This is especially true in the teaching of reading, where hearing children read individually has been the major teaching approach. Most teachers recognize the limitations of this. It is simply not possible to give sufficient one-to-one time to children in teaching reading to really ensure they all make progress.

In the literacy hour, children will spend about three-quarters of their time being taught as members of a whole class or a smaller ability group. Skilful use of class and group teaching can significantly increase the amount of active teaching time that children experience.

Another problem with literacy teaching in the past has been double counting, i.e. teachers would assume that because their children were writing in history, they must have been doing literacy work at the same time as history. The truth is that literacy needs teaching, not just practising.

Effective management of literacy at school level

Because the literacy hour is being adopted nationally it can provide a continuity of planning and teaching throughout the school which previously has been difficult to achieve.

For children, the literacy hour sets out common practices and predictable classroom routines that are carried forward when they move classes. When they enter a new class they have less learning of new routines to engage in and therefore enhanced time for learning literacy.

For teachers, the common structure of the literacy hour means that their planning can more easily be shared. It also gives a common basis for in-service training and means that teachers from different schools can collaborate in planning and training more effectively because they come with common assumptions and a shared language about how literacy should be taught.

For headteachers and school managers the literacy hour provides continuity in practice and the framework for continuing professional development of school staff.

Shared reading and writing at Key Stage 1

The place of these activities in the literacy hour

For the first fifteen minutes of the literacy hour the teacher works with the whole class. During this period the emphasis will be upon the sharing of a whole text with the class – either reading together an existing text, or collaboratively producing a new text. The texts involved will obviously need to be in a sufficiently large format for them to be seen clearly by all the children in the class.

An important part of shared reading and writing is the demonstrations given by the teacher of how reading and writing work. Some examples of the demonstrations the teacher might give are:

- reading aloud with fluency and expression from a text
- pointing to words and other text features such as full stops as she reads
- showing the class what she does when she comes to a new word – perhaps sounding the word out, or using the context to make a prediction about its meaning
- composing text and transcribing it in conventional ways
- drafting and revising what she writes as the ideas unfold
- checking her spelling of words, use of punctuation, etc.

A further aspect to shared reading and writing is the way these activities permit children gradually to become more and more involved in the reading and writing processes, but always to have the support of other collaborators. Such social support can help the development of confident and fluent reading and writing and lessens the chances of children failing in these crucial skills.

> Social learning is important. You might refer back to the teaching episodes discussed earlier for evidence of how this works.

The aims of these activities

Shared reading and writing have several aims:

- to provide a safe, communal environment in which aspects of reading and writing can be directly taught in an efficient way

- to enable a particular text to be revisited on several occasions with the class, gradually focusing upon more and more textual features

- to give the teacher opportunities to demonstrate to the class how reading and writing are done

- to give structured opportunities for children to take part in the shared text activity

- to enable children to be introduced to and interact with texts which are beyond their individual capabilities.

Points to bear in mind in shared reading

What kind of text to use?
You will need a range of enlarged texts, including stories, information texts and poetry, so that the children are able to see and hear text at the same time. These books should have a variety of formats, lively and interesting content and they should ideally be appropriate for extended use over three or four days in a week. Big Books are the most obvious

form of text to use, but it is possible to enlarge texts in other ways. Some texts can be enlarged up to A3 size using a photocopier. It is also possible to retype some texts on a word processor and then to print out this text at 48 point size. Some technological aids, such as an overhead projector, can also enlarge text.

What should be the level of difficulty of the texts?
The texts used should be within children's comprehension levels but, ideally, beyond the independent reading level of most of the class. They should therefore provide a challenge and be suitable for extending the children's skills.

If you have a mixed-age class, you will need to vary the difficulty levels of the texts used so that all children can experience an appropriate challenge on a regular basis but no children are continually at frustration level in the reading.

What is the teacher's role?
The teacher needs to take a number of roles:

- to read the text with (not simply to) the class

- to model early reading behaviours such as sound-symbol correspondence and directionality to teach basic concepts about print such as book, page, word, line, letter

- to teach and allow children to practise phonic- and word-recognition skills in context

- to show children how knowledge of sentence structures and punctuation can be useful reading strategies

- to monitor and check that children are reading for meaning

- to identify and correct errors as they occur

- to help children infer unknown words from the surrounding text and to confirm these by looking carefully at their spelling patterns

- to target teaching at a wide range of reading ability in the class by differentiating questions to stretch less able children as well as providing further reading opportunities and revision for others.

What is the child's role?
The child's role is to participate in the shared reading, individually and in unison, so as to learn and practise word and sentence level skills in the context of lively and interesting texts.

A useful resource can be laminated Big Books on which children and the teacher can write and then erase what they have written. It is possible to make your own laminated Big Books for this purpose.

Planning for shared writing

Points to bear in mind in shared writing

What kinds of texts might be written?
Any text type is amenable to being written collaboratively during a shared writing activity. To do this successfully you will need to use a whiteboard, large-format flipchart or overhead projector. It is particularly useful, however, in order to bring reading and writing closely together, to use shared reading texts as a starting point for shared writing. You might, for example:

- retell together a story you have recently read

- extend or finish a story you have read

- rework a story by substituting a character or by changing a setting

- use the text you have read to 'scaffold' or 'frame' the writing – e.g. substitute new rhymes in a rhyming story (invent some new dogs to accompany Hairy Maclary or add some new animals to the story of *The Grumpalump*); use a simple poem to write another in the same pattern ('Twinkle, twinkle, little cat ...'); write a recount using a simple writing frame ('First we ..., then we ... . Next ... . When we arrived we ... . Finally we ... .')

- use an extract from the text as a starting point, e.g. by carrying on from opening sentences, finishing off a section of dialogue

- write a new story round a familiar theme, e.g. new versions of fairy tales (read some of Roald Dahl's or Terry Jones' versions)

- find and record, in note form, information from the text you have read, then add further information to it.

What can be discussed with the children before, during and after shared writing?

Before writing

- discuss the audience for the writing – who do we want to read this (ourselves, younger children, a character in the story, the local policeman, parents)?

- discuss the tone of the writing – how should it sound (funny, scary, informative)?

- discuss the purpose of the writing – is it to amuse, to tell a story, to recount an experience, to give instructions, to explain, to remind, to summarize?

- brainstorm and note down ideas for the writing

- discuss the sequence of the writing and how it can be made clear.

While writing

Demonstrate and discuss:

- the difference between spoken and written language

- the direction and sequence of writing

- how to form sentences

- ways of joining sentences, e.g. 'and', 'also', 'before', 'when', 'so'

- agreement of tense, e.g. use of past tense for narratives

- the use of punctuation to mark sentences, speech, questions, lists

- layout – use of titles, headings, lists, paragraphs to organize meaning

- use of appropriate technical vocabulary, e.g. noun, verb, adjective

- spelling strategies, e.g. building words from known syllables and letter strings, spelling by analogy from known words or word parts, referring to words in text, dictionaries and/or word banks

These are similar to the points you would discuss with any child doing a writing activity. Shared writing makes it possible to discuss these so that all members of the class can benefit.

- noting and investigating new spelling patterns

- using new and alternative vocabulary for precision, to create effect, to avoid dullness and repetition

- using expressive and powerful language

- letter formation and consistency, upper and lower case, spacing between words

- using other presentation features, e.g. capitals and underlining for emphasis

- the features of different types of texts – style, grammar, language choices

- changing writing as you work, using editing marks to indicate changes

- adding, removing and reordering ideas.

- writing notes, asides and reminders for later inclusion or revision

- checking for sense by rereading as you write.

After writing

- reread the text with the class to discuss and improve its clarity, effect, suitability for purpose and audience

- edit to improve the text – use editing marks or rewrite as appropriate

- proof-read, checking for accuracy – grammar, punctuation and spelling

- discuss the presentation of the writing, e.g. how might it be displayed and used subsequently?

What you will need for shared reading and writing
Typically you will work with the class sitting in front of you on a carpeted area. Sit facing the class with the Big Book open on a bookstand or easel beside you. You might find a pointer useful for indicating particular details in the book. You will also find it useful to have at one side a writing-board (a portable whiteboard, a flipchart or a piece of large paper clipped to a painting easel).

Big Books

Using the Big Book
A Big Book might be used every day for a week. A new Big Book can be introduced on a Monday and then the same Big Book used for shared reading every day until the end of the week. Then, on the following Monday, you might introduce a new Big Book for that week. The reason for using the same Big Book over a whole week is that the children's increasing familiarity with the text will enable them to explore the text in more challenging ways as the week progresses.

> Don Holdaway first suggested the concept of the Big Book in 1979 in his book *Foundations of Literacy*.

What do you do with the Big Book?
The discussion you will have with the children about the Big Book, the questions you ask them and the features of the text that you explain

will be determined by the learning objectives you have selected for that week. Of course you will have to pick your Big Book so as to make sure that you have got a text that fits in with those objectives. This is not as difficult as it sounds – most good Big Books will be helpful for a very wide range of learning objectives.

How does the shared reading/writing vary over a week?
In a typical week with a Big Book you might do the following:

Monday
Introduce this week's Big Book (*Not Now Bernard* by David McKee) to the class. Show them the front cover and ask them to identify the title and the author. Ask the children what they think this story might be about. Show the children some of the illustrations and ask them to comment on these. Then read the book through to the children, using the pointer to indicate the words as you read. You might stop every now and then and ask the children to predict what is going to happen next in the story. At the end of the book ask for their responses to the story and finally read the story through again using the pointer. Some children will be able to join in this time and you should encourage and praise this.

Tuesday
Begin by reading the story again to the class. The growing familiarity with the text should mean that many children will be able to read along with you. After this initial reading, ask children questions which enable them to relate the text to their own experience, e.g. 'If you were Bernard what would you have done to make someone listen to you?'

Then draw the children's attention to the word 'ROAR' on a page halfway through the book. Through discussion and explanation establish that the word is printed differently from other words on the page – it is all in capital letters. You will need to employ further question and explanation to establish the purpose of this use of capitals. Here it is used to emphasize the word and to ensure that it is read loudly and fiercely. You might then contrast this with the title of the book as printed on the cover. This is also in capitals. Through question and explanation establish that this is a different use of capitals and that titles are often, although not always, printed in capital letters.

Wednesday
Turn to the page where the monster is breaking one of Bernard's toys. The text says 'And broke one of his toys'. Previously you should have covered up the last word with a Post-it. Ask the children what the covered-up word might be. Several children should remember the word and you can either write the word yourself on the writing board or you can ask one of the children to come out and write it for you. Then uncover the word and ask the children to check if they had got it right. Then cover up the word again and ask the children to suggest some other words that would fit – that is, would still make sense. When the children suggest alternatives you can add these to the list on the board. Then tell the children that they are going to read the book again, but this time when they come to that covered word in the book they are going to use one of the new words they have suggested instead. Help the children to select one of the new words and write it on a Post-it and fix it in the right place. Then reread the book from the beginning (using the pointer) but including the substituted word in the appropriate place.

Thursday

Start the session by reading the book together with the whole class. Try to make this a brisk and expressive reading. After this turn back to the page where Bernard's father says 'Not now, Bernard'. Tell the children that they are going to add something to the story. Bernard's father is going to explain to Bernard why he can't listen to him now. Ask the children to suggest different sentences. For example: 'Not now, Bernard. I am busy', 'Not now, Bernard. I am hammering a nail', and so on. As these sentences are suggested either write them on the board yourself or ask children to come out to write them. Even if you write them yourself you may ask the class how to spell particular words, or prompt for reminders about capital letters and full stops. Your final stimulus to the class might be to ask them to think of a sentence that could be written in capital letters (reminding them of what they learned on Tuesday about the use of capital letters for emphasis or exclamation).

Friday

Show the class the front cover of the book and ask the children to describe the monster illustrated there. Record all or some of their suggestions on the board. You might do this yourself or ask individual children to come out to do it. Then read the book through together for one last time. Remind the children that a normal-size copy of *Not Now Bernard* is available for them to read by themselves in the classroom.

> This sequence can readily be adapted for other shared texts. Revisiting a text is important as it allows children to focus on particular aspects of reading at particular times.

Shared reading and writing with Key Stage 2 children

In Key Stage 2 the first fifteen minutes are again used to work with the whole class on a shared text. This may be a Big Book. Teachers are most familiar with Big Books written for younger readers but publishers are increasingly producing Big Books that contain challenging reading and are aimed at an older audience.

Beyond the Big Book

Although there are some Big Books available that could be used with children up to Year 6, teachers will need to use other sources of text as well. By Key Stage 2 these shared reading and writing sessions will need to look at a wide range of texts – poems, advertisements, newspaper articles, short extracts from novels, etc. Big Books are not likely in themselves to meet the demand for such a wide range of reading material.

In any case some Key Stage 2 teachers will not be able to use Big Books because the physical constraints of their classrooms will not enable all the children to sit together in an area where they can all have a good view of a Big Book.

So, for one reason or another, Key Stage 2 teachers will need to have other strategies for sharing texts with their classes. There are a number of such strategies:

• You might be able to copy short straightforward texts by hand on to a whiteboard or blackboard.

• You might also make each child a photocopy of the chosen text or extract.

• If you have access to an overhead projector you can make OHP transparencies from the original text.

- You might be able to enlarge a text or extract on the photocopier.

- By typing a text into a word processor you will be able to print it out with a font size of around 48 points – big enough for the class to read.

Whatever strategies are used it is important that all children have sufficiently clear sight of the text to read it for themselves. It is not sufficient in these sessions for children to have heard the text read to them.

> Experience has suggested the 'fifteen foot' test for shared texts – if you can read the text clearly from fifteen feet away, it is big enough for a class to work with together.

Do older children study the same text every day for a week?

You do not need to plan shared reading sessions this way. Younger children, for example up to Year 4, might well benefit from revisiting the same text over the five days. By using the same text over a whole week the children's increasing familiarity with it will enable them to explore it in more challenging ways as the week progresses.

Teachers of older children may choose to use the same text every day for a week. They may also choose to use a particular text for two or three consecutive days before moving on the next day to something different such as a text of a similar type or a further extract of the same text. The richer the text the more likely you are to want to use it for several days in a row.

How does the teacher do shared reading/writing with older pupils?

A typical sequence of shared reading/writing sessions with a Year 5–6 class might be organized as follows:

Text type for this term: biography and autobiography

Text for this sequence of lessons: an extract from *War Boy* by Michael Foreman

Learning objectives, taken from the National Literacy Strategy framework of objectives:
- to help children distinguish between fact, opinion, fiction and commentary
- to develop children's skills of biographical and autobiographical writing in role
- to help children distinguish between implicit and explicit points of view
- to engage the class in researching the origins of proper names, e.g. place names and names of products

Day 1

Tell the class the title of the book from which the extract has been chosen. Ask for suggestions about what the book might be about. After some initial responses tell them that the book has a subtitle 'A country childhood'. Ask them what effect this has on their expectations of what the book 's content might be. Give out individual photocopies of pages 54 and 55, which contain a description of some air raids. Read the text aloud. You might choose to read it to the class yourself, choose a child to do it, or ask different children to read different paragraphs. Then check their understanding by asking questions. What sort of writing is